Composing Made Easy

by Gail Smith

www.melbay.com

CONTENTS

Chapter One..................................What's in a Name..4

Chapter Two..................................Take Five...9

Chapter Three..............................Pentatonic Scale Songs...............................13

Chapter Four.................................Five - Tone Blues..18

Chapter Five..................................Whole –Tone Melody..................................21

Chapter Six.....................................Musical Q & A...24

Chapter Seven...............................Song Form..26

Chapter Eight.................................Using a Poem to Compose........................28

Chapter Nine..................................Inspired by Nature.....................................31

Chapter Ten....................................Palindromes and Semordnilaps.................34

Chapter Eleven..............................Inverted Songs..37

Chapter Twelve..............................Twelve –Tone Songs....................................38

Amy Beach's Ten Commandments for Composers...40

Preface

Anything can be easy if you enjoy what you are doing and know what you are doing. This book was written to help you see what you can do by showing vivid examples of a variety of ways to compose. Step by step you will be able to write a melody, add rhythm and then add harmony using a left hand pattern.

The mystery surrounding composers will always abound, and in no way do I wish to imply or diminish the rare genius of Mozart and other great composers. However, there are some simple ways to start the process of composition. The more musically advanced you are, obviously, it will enable you to compose more difficult music. Often the most simple, subtle melody is remembered and loved more than the most difficult piece ever composed. Everyone may not have the talent to compose a symphony, yet everyone really can compose a melody if they try. Everything begins with a short motif or melody.

The more we see and experience, the more we can imagine. Your imagination sparks ideas that you may put into musical notes. Close your eyes and imagine something incredible, something beautiful or some exotic place you would like to visit. Imagination and inspiration go hand in hand. Soon you may be able to describe your experience musically.

There is a wonderful preserve called Roxborough Park near Denver, Colorado. I spent several hours walking through this incredible park. It was an awesome and inspiring experience. There was one especially beautiful bird call which I wrote down and used as a melody for a new song.

These words were inscribed on a sign at the entrance to the park:

I stroll through a symphony for my senses, textures, sounds, and smells harmonize with my own heartbeat.
I feel part of the very pulse of the earth. Being quiet within myself, I am open to the melodies.
The flute-Like solo of the Canyon wren, the harsh staccato of the scrub jay,
the subtle verse of summer chorus, frogs or crackling winter ice.
The startling snare-drum of the occasional rattle snake, and the harmonies.
Acrid odor of fox, vibrant blue of sky suspended above rocks of every red surprisingly rich texture of multicolored stone,
prickly plant leaves and cool smooth aspen bark, masses of lady bugs, and twilight, filled with twinkling fireflies.

As you consider ideas for songs, be inspired by the beauty of nature around you, the rain, the sky and hopefully the ideas in this book will spark the creativity in you.

Let's get started now! Have fun on your musical journey as a composer.

Best wishes,

GAIL SMITH

Chapter One

What's in a Name

Review the lines and spaces. Now we will take the musical letters found in your name to compose a melody. Taking the name, Celia Alexandra, as an example, you see that there are eight musical letters to use in her name. First I will place these letters on the treble cleff staff; then give a rhythm to the notes. Next I'll find a chord that includes notes from the melody that will blend or harmonize with that melody. Now write your name out and find the musical letters in it. Draw the notes in the treble clef staff and try using the musical letters in your name to compose "The Name Song."

The Musical Alphabet is

a b c d e f g

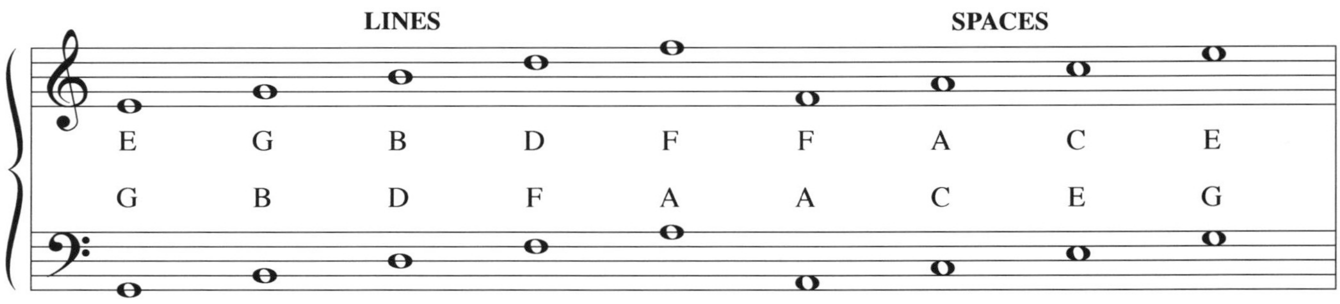

Find the musical letters in your name,
then draw them in the staff below

Composing a Name Song
Step by Step

Celia Alexandra

1. Find the musical letters and place them in the treble clef

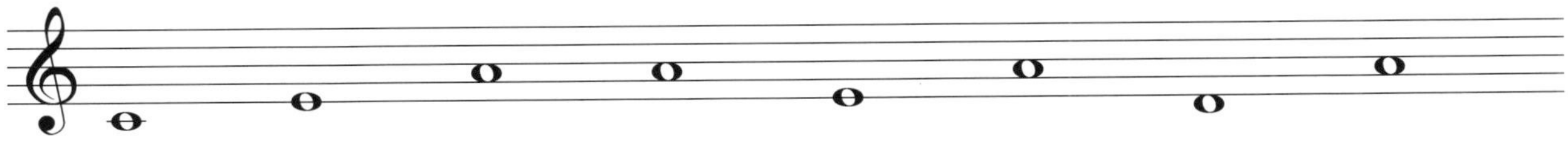

2. Give the notes a rhythm

3. Try another time signature

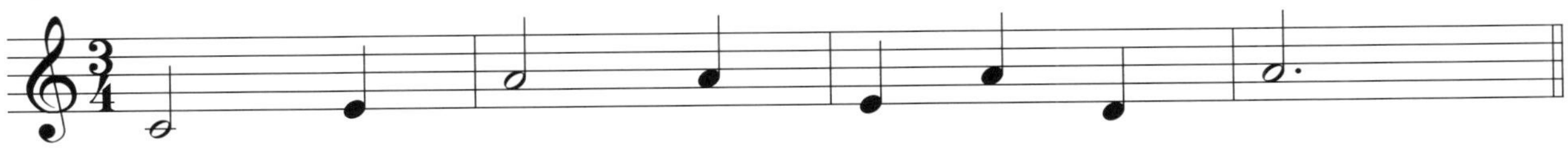

4. Change the position of the notes on the staff

5. Add a chord in the bass clef

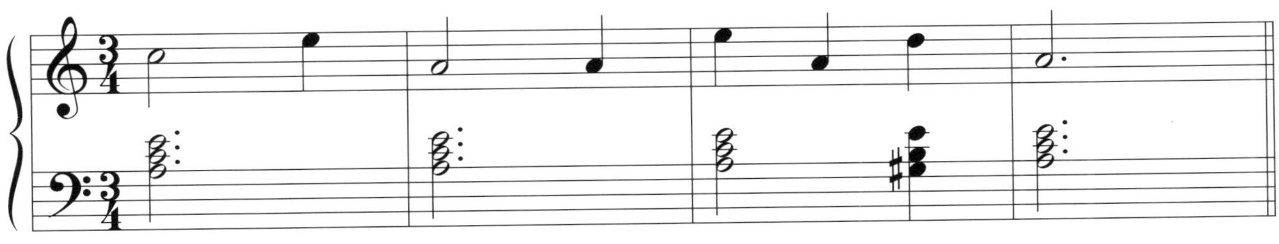

6. Change the song to a major key

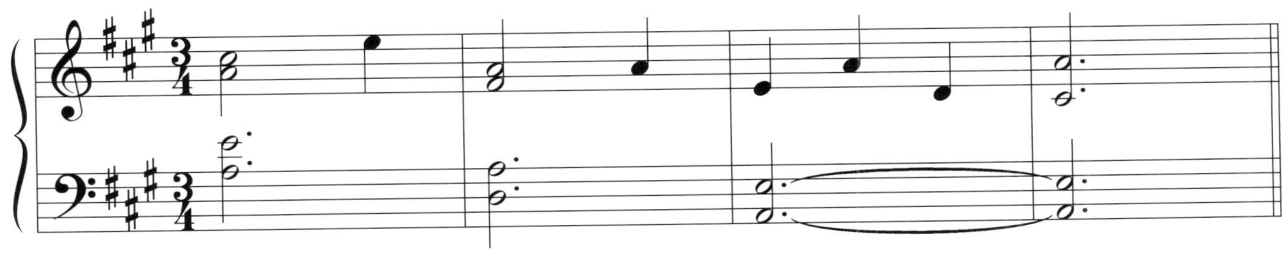

7. **Try adding notes in between the melody to keep the song growing**

8. **Harmonize the melody note with a chord**

9. **Reharmonize in 4-part harmony in the major key**

10. **Add left hand auxiliary notes from the scale**

11. **Place the melody in the bass clef**

12. **Chime**

Celia's Song

Gail Smith

Moderato

A classical piano solo composed by Robert Schumann that used the musical letters in his friend's name.

Norse Song

Composed in honor of the Danish composer, Niels W. Gade (1817-1890)

This composition uses the musical letters in Gade's name.

Robert Schumann
Op. 68, No. 41

Chapter Two

Take Five

A melody may be formed by using a pattern of five numbers. Using the first five numbers, 1-2-3-4-5, there are 120 different patterns that can be formed. Take the number 1 and have it correspond with the note C, the number 2 is D, 3 is E, 4 is F, and 5 is G. I have picked the group of five numbers in this order: 5-1-4-3-2. The corresponding notes are G-C-F-E-D. The melody is then given a rhythm and a song is born. There are several rhythms that I will notate for you so you see a few of the possible ways the melody could have gone.

Select a Number

5 1 4 3 2

Now choose a rhythm

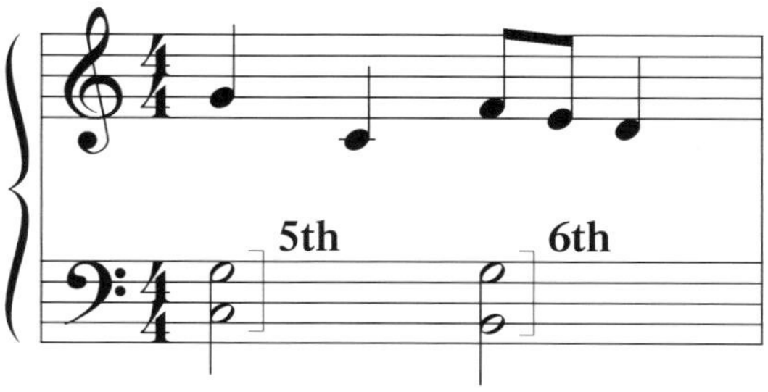

or

Higher:

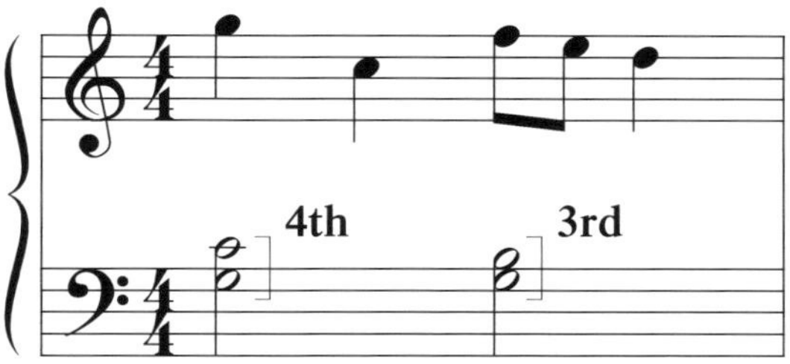

or

Alternate the pattern between the hands:

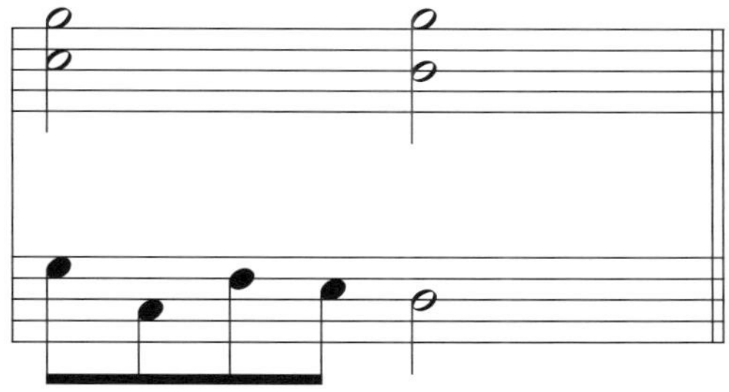

Here are six other rhythmic possibilities:

The Pattern Becomes a Musical Piece

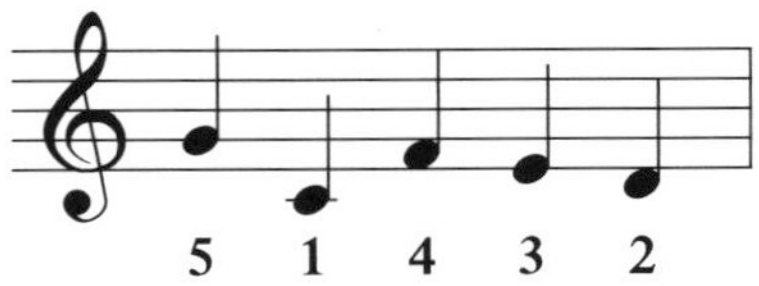

Gail Smith

Now it should be clear to see how to compose a musical piece starting with only five numbers, and then changing those numbers into musical notes.

Assignment:
Compose your own song using the pattern 5 1 4 3 2.

Adding Chords to the Pattern

This eight-measure piece uses the pattern 5 3 4 2 1
with four different chords.

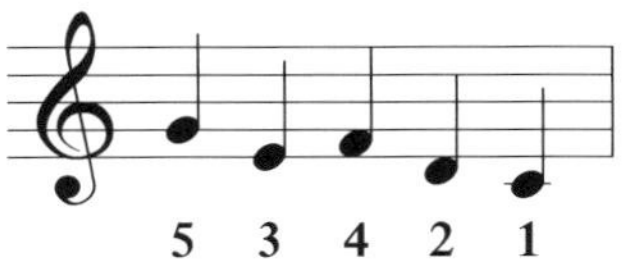

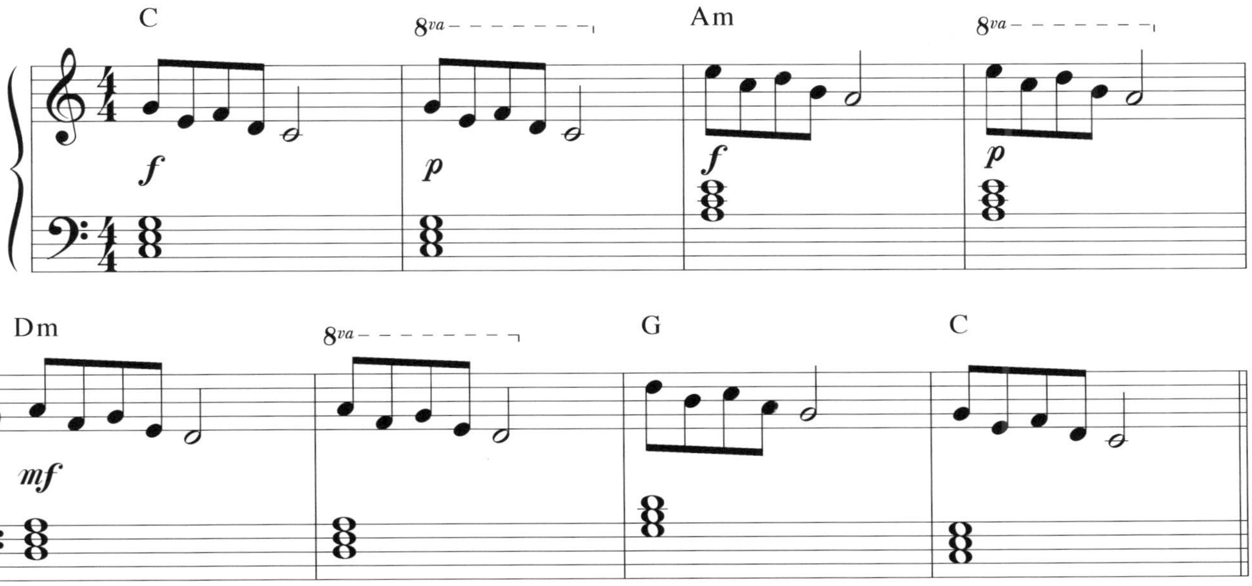

Now improvise or compose another pattern, then
fill in each measure below with that pattern.

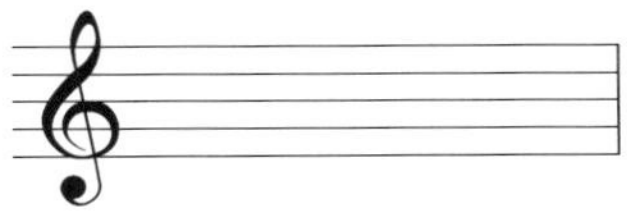

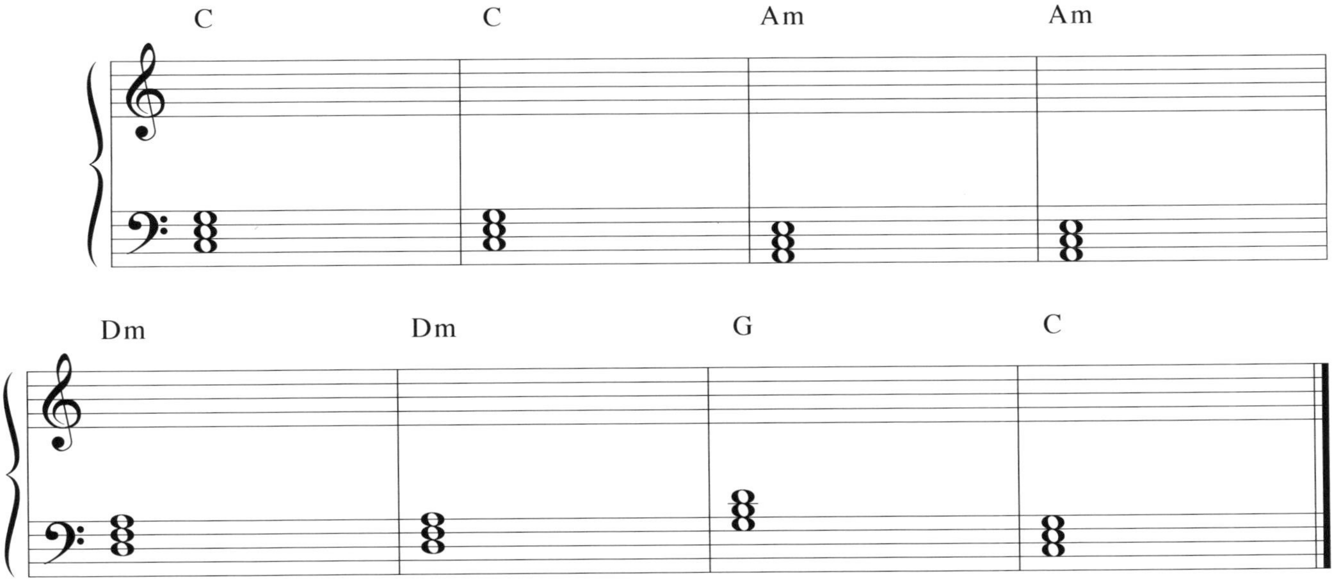

Dreaming
(My Favorite Pattern)

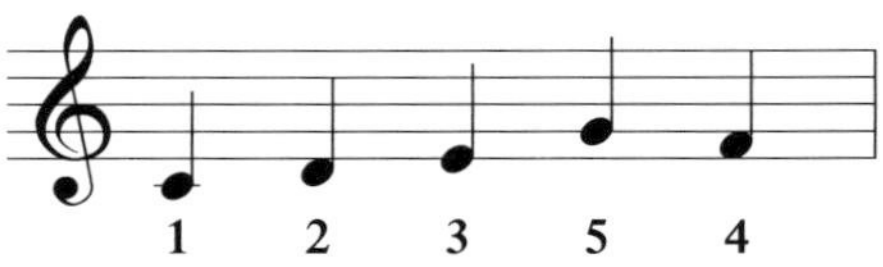

Gail Smith

Chapter Three

Pentatonic Scale Songs

The pentatonic scale is made up using the five black notes on the piano. First play just the pattern 1-2-3-4-5 and start on each of the black keys and listen to the different melody that is produced when you play 1-2-3-4-5 on each of the black keys. Five different tunes are created. Play the group of black notes with another set of the 120 five-note patterns. Start again and mix up the order of the black keys first with the group of the two black keys and then the group of three black keys as a starting point for the five numbers. The result is having five different melodies using the same five numbers but each one has a different sound starting on each one of the black keys.

Five Tones (There are 120 ways to play 5 tones)

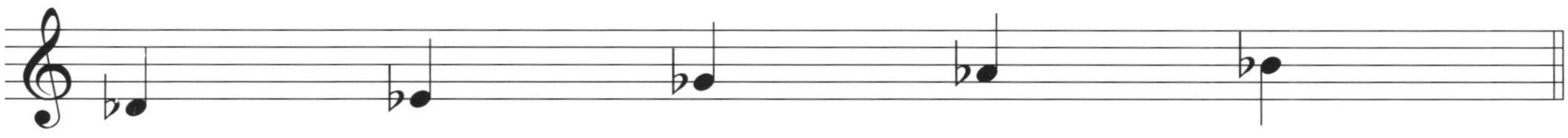

Ex. 1

Create Indian Music

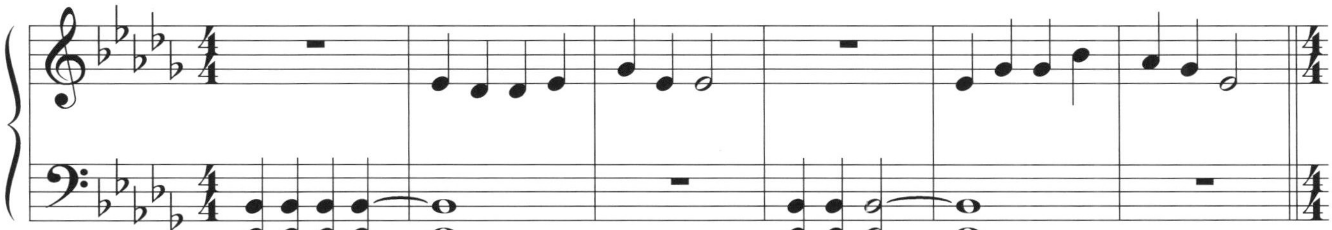

Ex. 2

Create Oriental Music

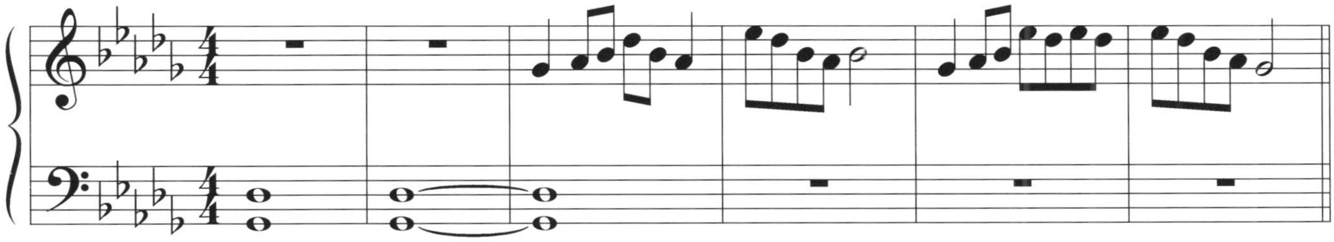

Ex. 3

Imitate Bagpipes

Black Key Patterns

Play and listen to the unique sounds made by using the 1 2 3 5 4 pattern starting on each of the black keys. Each pattern creates a lovely melody waiting for a rhythm to give it a life as a new musical piece.

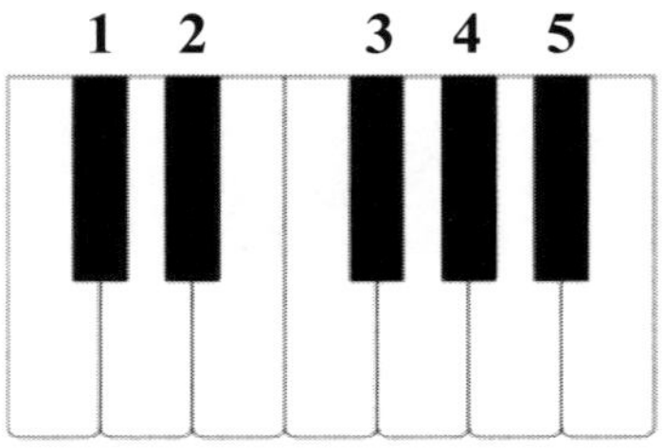

Starting on Db

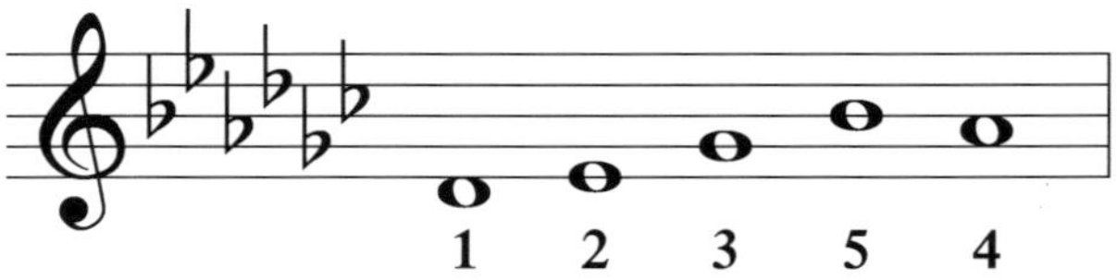

Starting on Eb

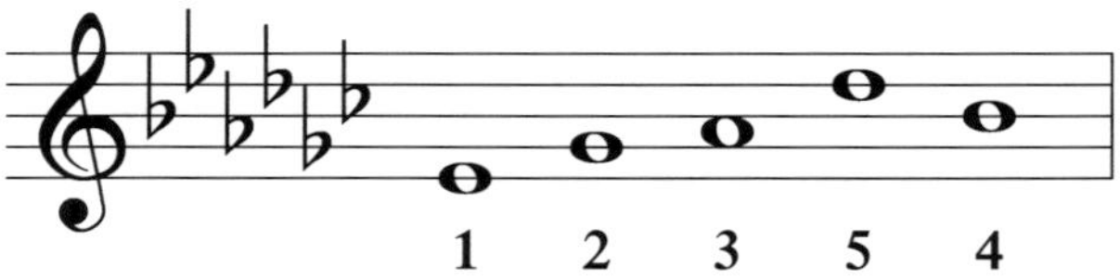

Starting on Gb

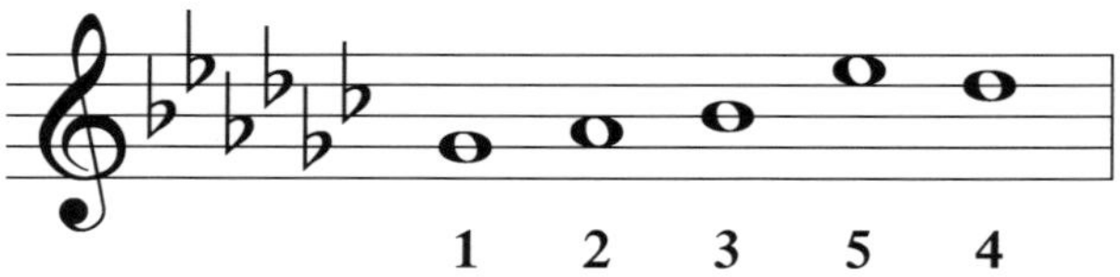

Starting on Ab

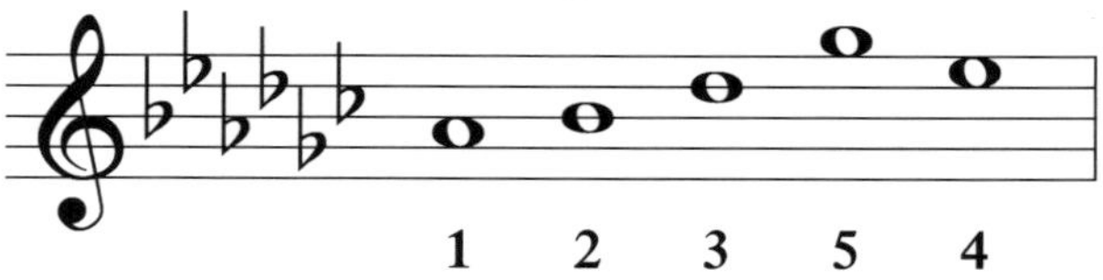

Starting on Bb

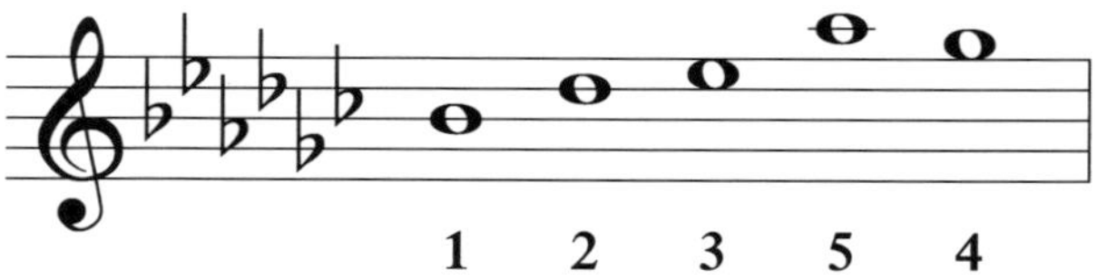

Pentatonic Mutations

One pattern inverted on each note of the pentatonic scale explodes into 25 different sound patterns.

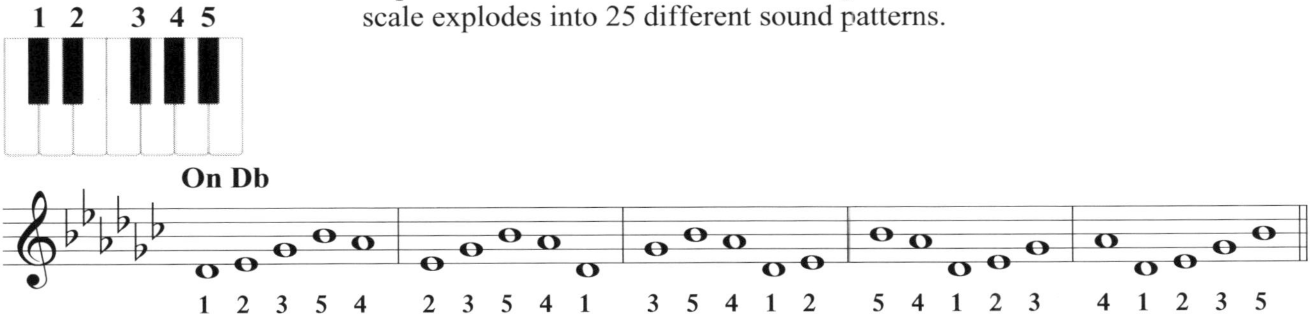

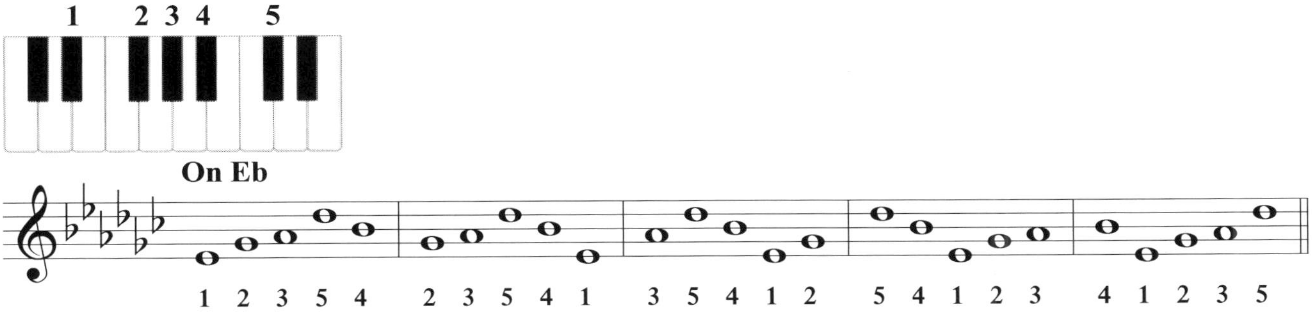

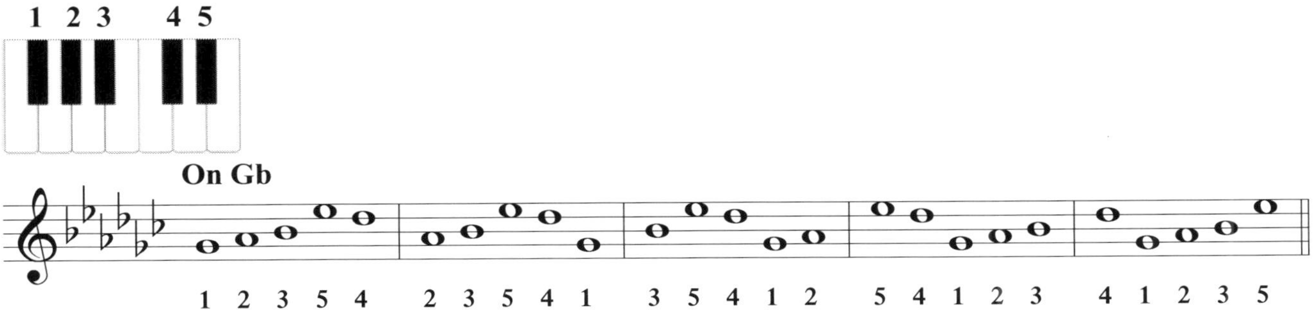

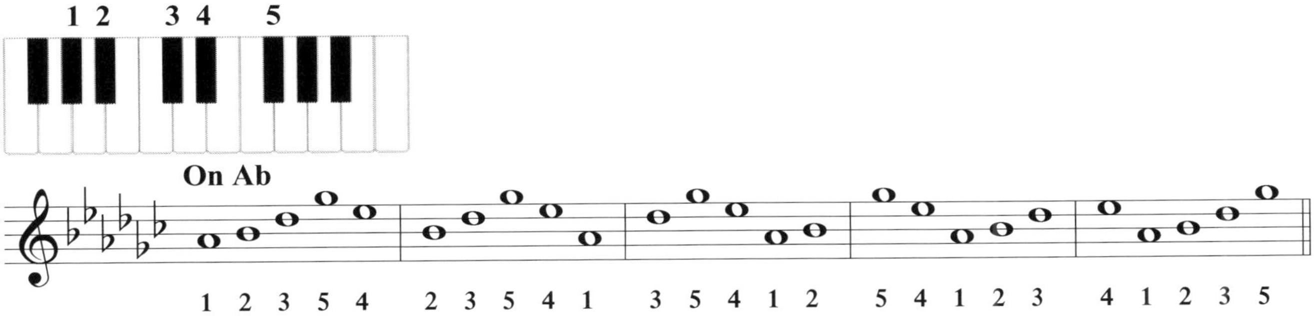

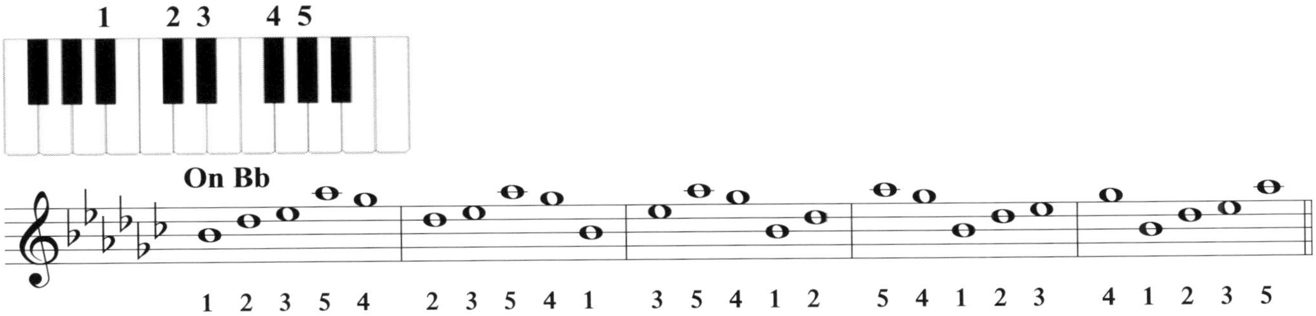

Using the Pattern 1 2 3 5 4 on the Black Keys

Gail Smith

Half and Half

Improvising on the black keys is enjoyable, relaxing, and brings out your creativity.
Please finish the second phrase on each line.

Imagine you are having a musical conversation,
speaking a question followed by an answer.

Chapter Four

Five-Tone Blues

Still using a pattern of five numbers, try this new set of five-note-blues scales as your notes from your number sequence. Number 1 is C, 2 is Eb, 3 is F, 4 is Gb, 5 is G natural. The chart on the page will show you how to form each blues scale on different starting notes. First use the number pattern, 1-2-3-4-5. Using just these notes from the five-note-blues scales, many cool jazz riffs can be composed. Repeat parts of the groups of five or take three notes from the group as I did in measure eleven of the piece, "Light Jazz."

5-Finger Blues Pattern on C **Retrograde** **Random Pattern**

5-Finger Blues Pattern on D

5-Finger Blues Pattern on E

5-Finger Blues Pattern on F

5-Finger Blues Pattern on G

Light Jazz

(Using 5-Finger Blues Patterns)

Gail Smith

Now compose a Twelve-Bar Blues song
using the 5-Finger Blues Patterns

Chapter Five

Whole-Tone Melody

Compose an impressionistic song using the whole tone scales. There are two of these scales: one starts on C and another one starts on Db. Each scale has six notes in it. Using six numbers now to create a melody, can you believe there are 720 different combinations of six notes that you can create! Let the number 1 represent the note C, 2 is D, 3 is E; then 4 is F#, 5 is G#, 6 is A#. The song may sound like waterfalls, rain, underwater adventures or swimming in the ocean. Repeat your number phrase over and over, and then try another pattern of numbers. The results can be as long as a river. Have fun! Your piece will look harder written down than if you just improvise this whole-tone scale. Play a while, then write some down.

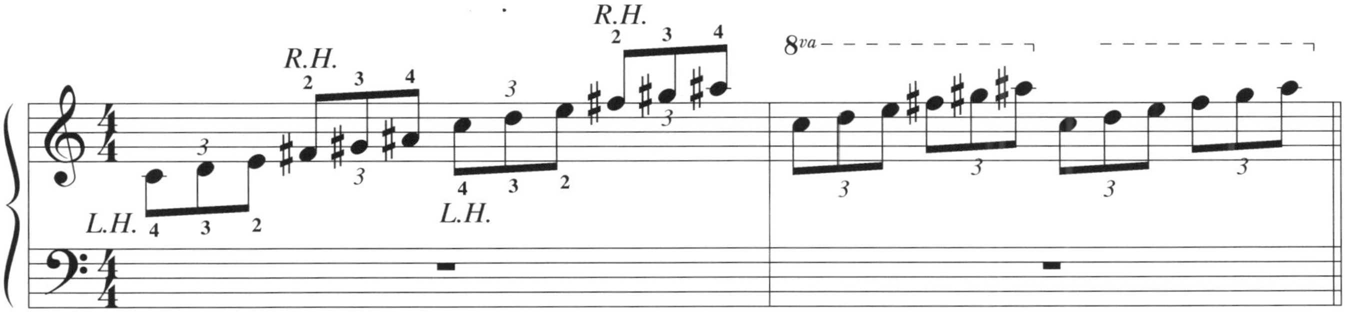

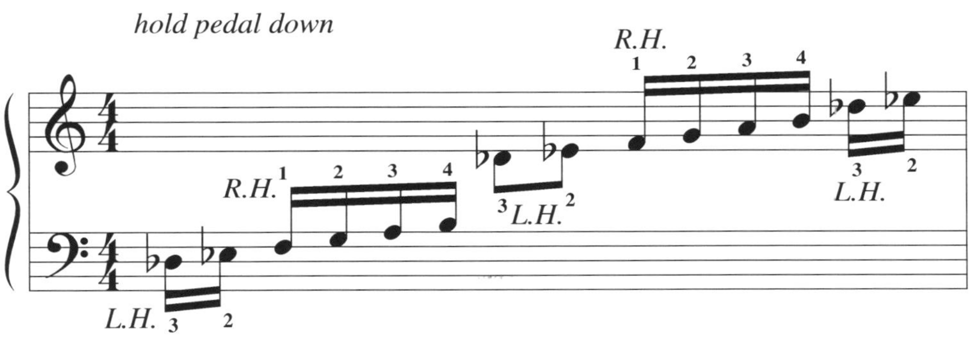

Whole Tone Clusters

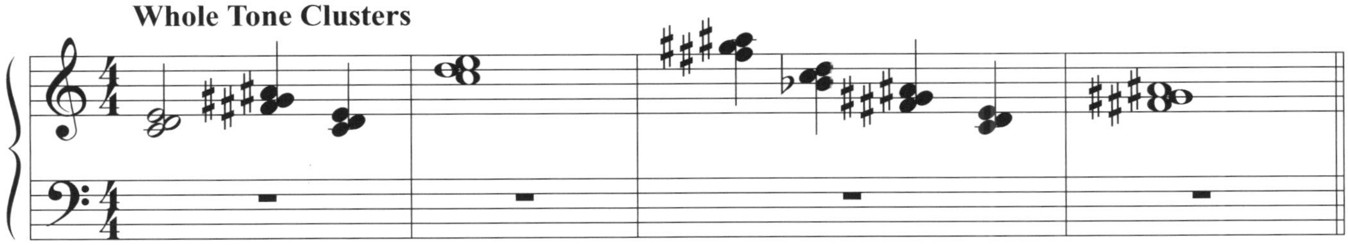

Play the Whole Tone Scale after an Augmented Chord

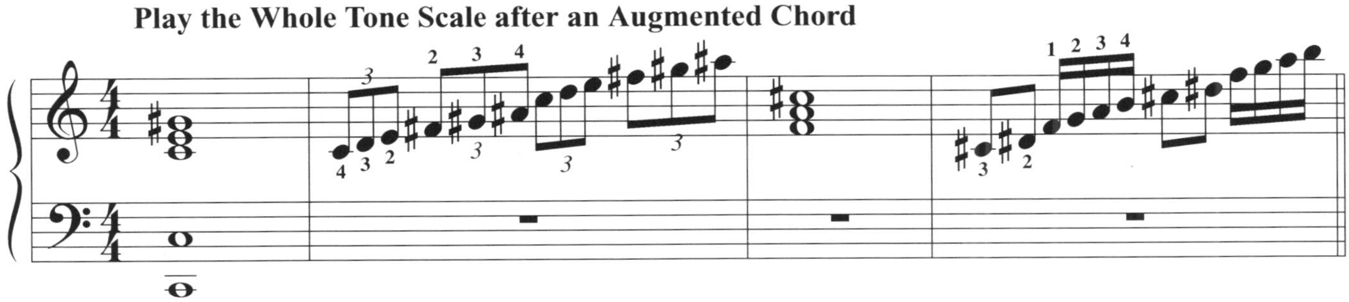

Here are 12 ways to play 6 notes.

Compose 8 more ways.

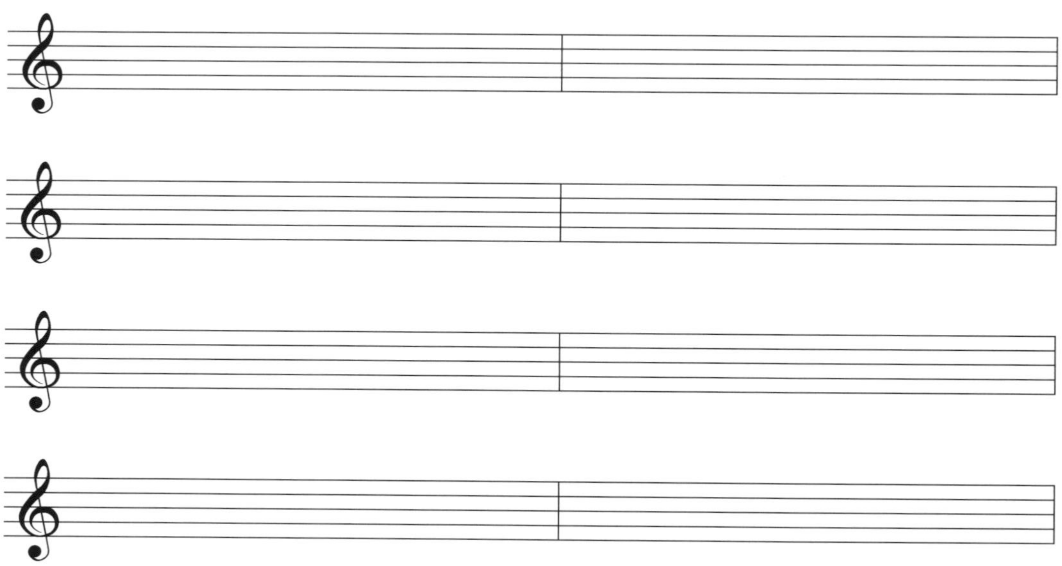

Waterfalls in Oregon

(composed using the Whole-Tone Scale)

Gail Smith

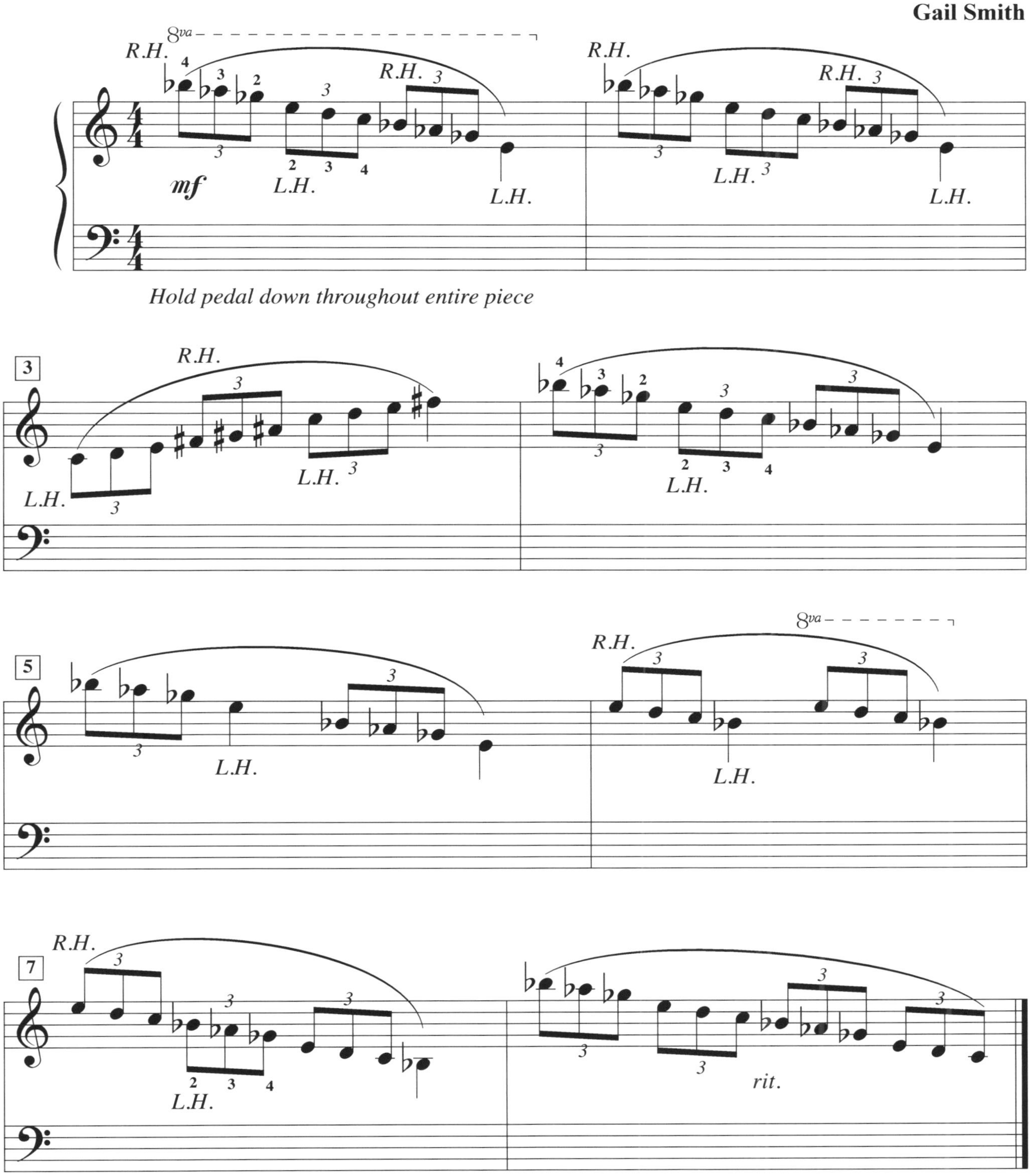

Chapter Six

Musical Q & A

Composing is a lot like having a conversation with someone. The friend asks a question and then you give an answer. Your answer can be simply another group of five notes. The rhythm of your conversation can turn into notes. Pitch the notes as you speak them. You don't talk in monotones like a robot, so think how the words go, either higher or lower as the inflection of your voice rises and falls. Say the word potato chip several times and then imagine how weird it would be to break up each syllable and pronounce it: pooo-taaa-tooo chip. Some melodies just have to move along to make musical sense just like saying potato all together makes English sense.

Here's a famous example of two phrases

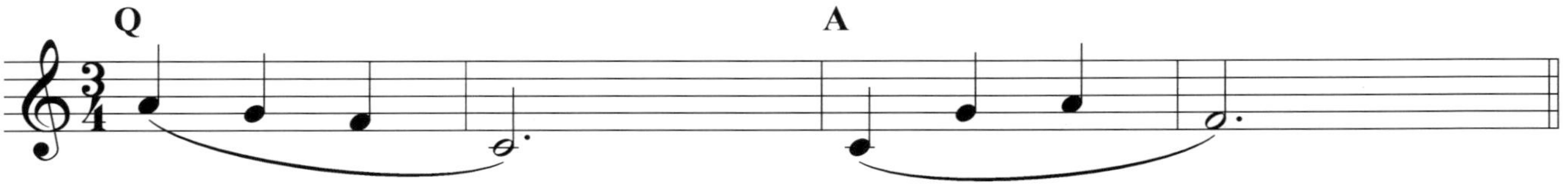

Fill in your answer to these musical questions.

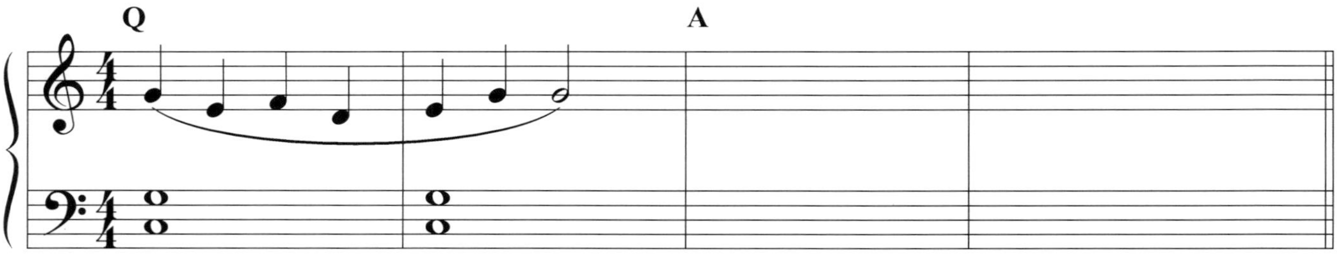

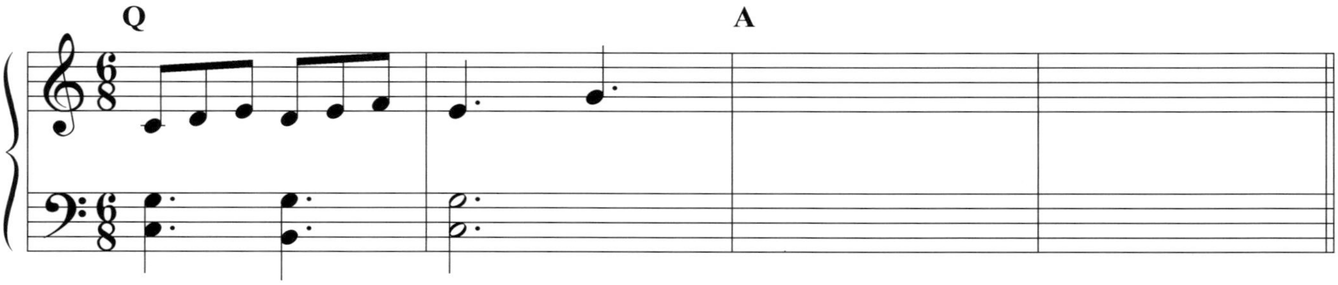

Assignment: write musical questions and answers

Chapter Seven

Song Form
(Forming Melodic Phrases)

The melody must conform to some musical form just as several sentences form a paragraph. A melodic fragment needs to grow to form a longer musical phrase usually of four musical measures. Look at the example of the simple song "Hot Cross Buns." The simple melody forms a pattern of AABA of just one measure each. Now compare that to the AABA pattern of the longer song, "Joyful, Joyful, We Adore Thee." Each section is four measures in length with the whole song being 16 measures.

Hot Cross Buns

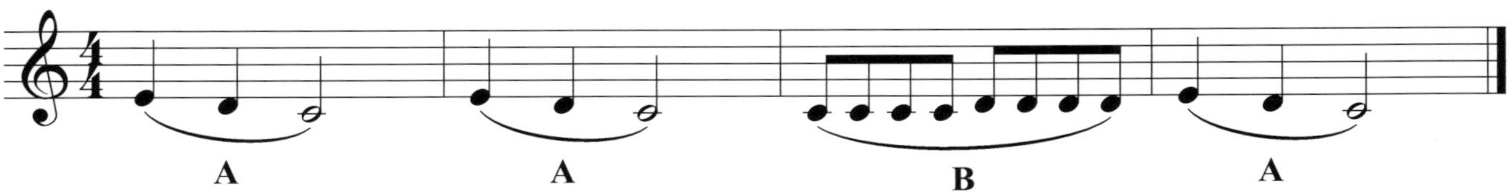

Joyful, Joyful, We Adore Thee

One of the basic ideas in musical form is that of symmetry or balance. As a rule, the initial phrase of a hymn is balanced by an answering phrase; the first is called the antecedent phrase; the second is called the consequent phrase. The first phrase states a musical idea and the second follows in consequence. These two related phrases are called a period. A double period consists of four phrases.

The following hymn will be an example of a double period (16 measures).

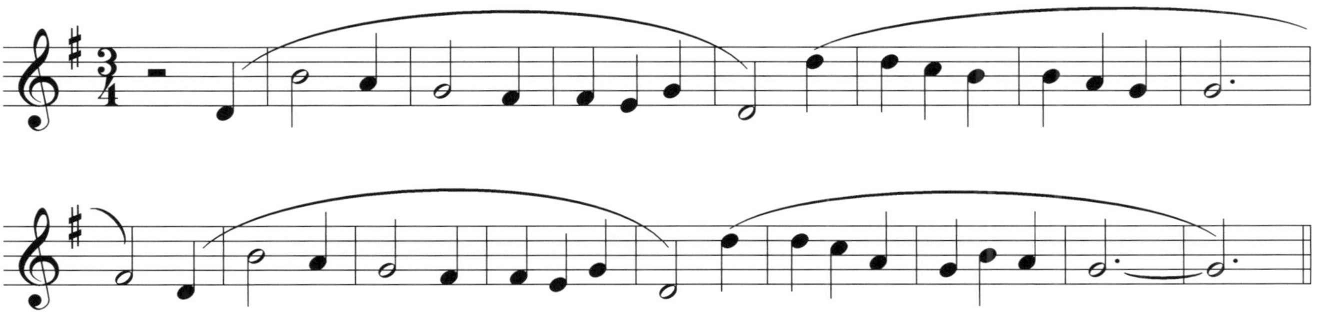

There is no strict rule as to phrase-length; three-measure and five-measure phrases do occur in hymns. The following hymn phrases are examples of some of the irregular phrases.

2-measure phrase

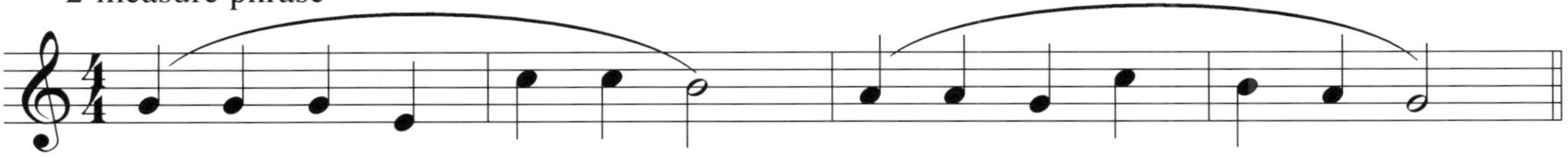

3-measure phrase

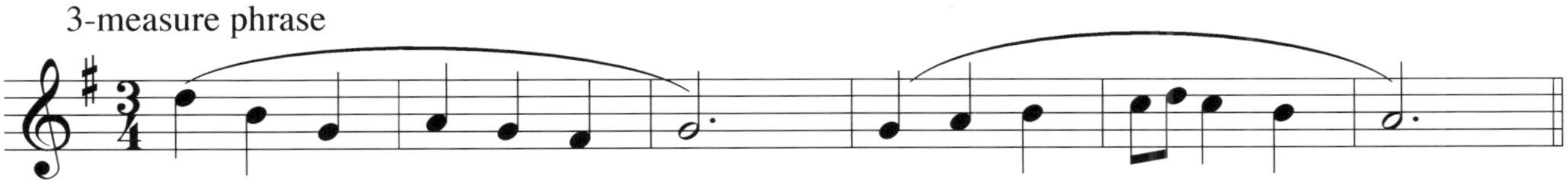

4-measure phrase

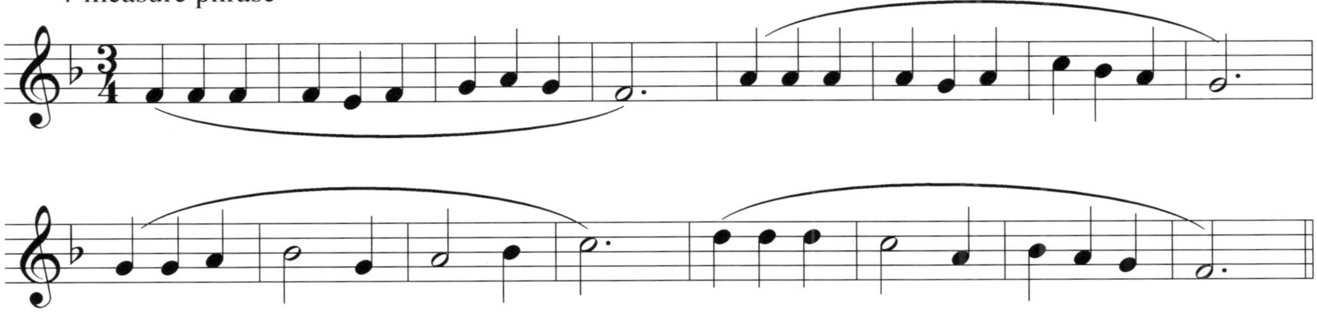

5-measure phrase

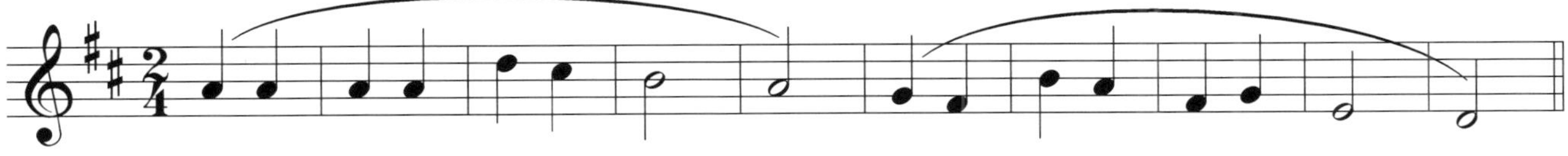

Chapter Eight

Using a Poem to Compose

Many composers have been inspired to create a melody to the words of a poem. When selecting a poem, think of the meter of the syllables in each line. At first it will be easy to have a different note for each syllable. There are poems that have 8 syllables to a phrase, some have 6. Long Meter has four phrases that each have 8 syllables. Short Meter has 6 6 8 6, Common Meter has 8 6 8 6 (eight syllables in the first phrase and six syllables in the second phrase).

Read this poem:

God, grant me the serenity
To accept the things I cannot change,
The courage to change the things I can,
And the wisdom to know the difference.

Next, a rhythm:

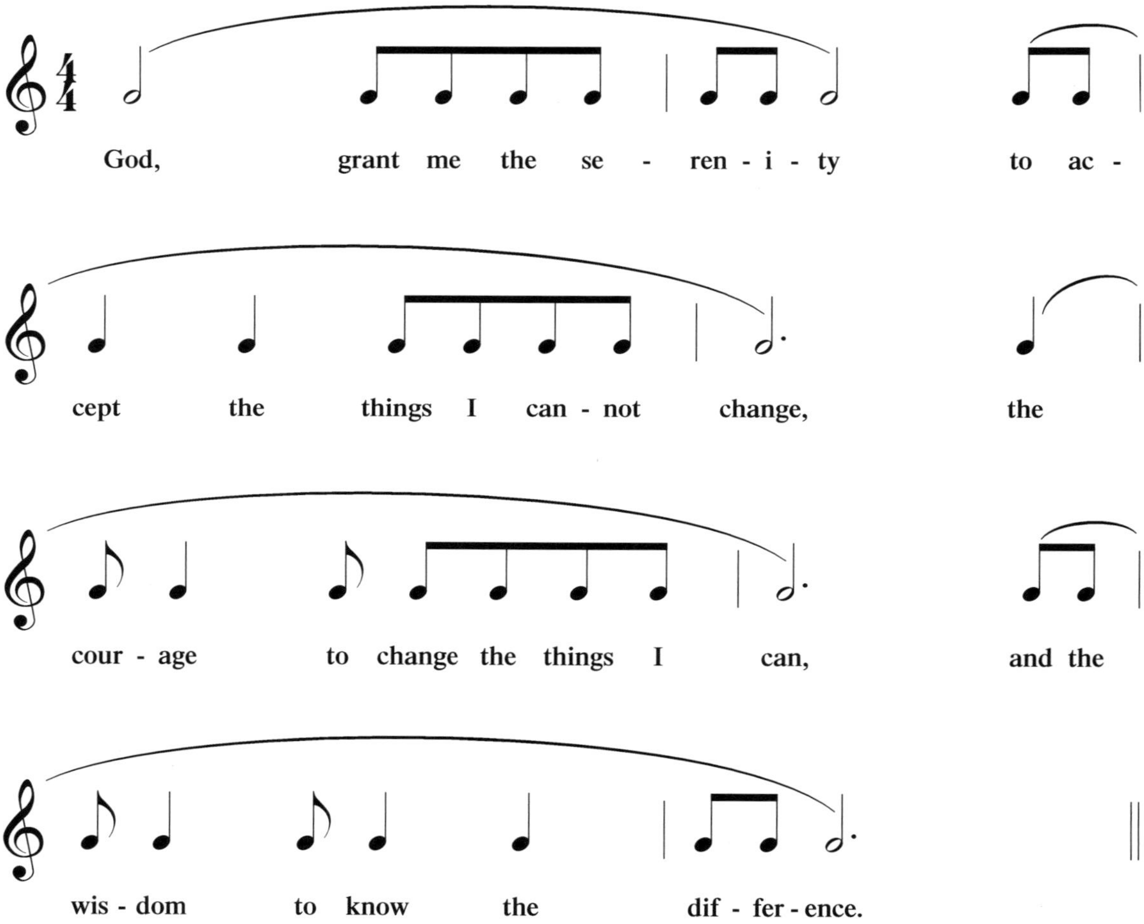

The result: 4 phrases, 8 measures.

Five Steps to Setting a Poem to Music

STEP ONE

What is the purpose of your song? Find a need and fill it. Select a special poem or text for a solo or choir.

STEP TWO

Checklist for the text:
1. Count the number of phrases
2. Count the number of syllables in each phrase
3. Determine what meter it is in

CM (Common Meter) is a convenient way of saying there are eight syllables in lines one and three, and six syllables in lines two and four – or 86.86.
Example:__________________

LM (Long Meter) is 88.88.
Example:__________________

SM (Short Meter) is 66.86.
Example:__________________

STEP THREE

1. Determine the natural rhythm of the words by repeating the text over and over.
2. Trace the inflection of the syllables.
3. Have the melody follow the natural inflection of words.
4. Be sure to have the placement of the noun and verb on the strong beat (beats one and three).

Repeat each phrase aloud until you have the natural rhythm of the words with the most beautiful reading of the text possible.

STEP FOUR

Notate the rhythm. Here are the nine basic units of rhythm.

STEP FIVE

Using the twelve tones and the song forms AABA, ABAC, ABABAC, just allow the music to happen. Be patient.

Here is a melody using the rhythm given.

Now compose your melody that flows with the rhythm of the words in the poem.

Chapter Nine

Inspired by Nature

Everything around us has the potential to inspire us. A beautiful rainbow, a pretty rose, a lovely river or lake, the ocean waves, a sailboat, and thousands of other sights. Sounds from nature can inspire us as well. The sounds of the surf, thunder, rain, crickets, bird calls, and soe many other pleasant sounds and noises. With that it mind, take a walk outside and listen for a sound that either gives you a special beat or the sound of a bird call. Some evening you may try going outside and looking at the stars and see the distance between the stars in the Big Dipper and write a song, or be inspired by the moon. I was inspired by a bird song of just three notes. The three notes were repeated in equal time spans that lasted for seven minutes. Here is the actual bird song with the harmony that seemed to go with it.

Mystery Bird

Gail Smith

A Hermit Thrush at Morn

(Op. 92, No. 2)

"I heard from morn to morn a merry thrush
Sing hymns of rapture, while I drank the sound
With Joy." — J. Clare

Amy Marcy Beach (1867-1944)

Quasi Valse Lento

* **These bird calls are exact notations of the Hermit Thrush songs heard by Amy Beach at the MacDowell Colony, Peterborough, N.H.**

Listen for a bird call and compose a song based on the bird call.

Chapter Ten

Palindromes and Semordnilaps

A Palindrome is something that is the same backwards or forward. When composing backwards, it is called a retrograde. You can use the first two phrases of a song and then write them again going backwards so that when it is played it will be the same either way.

The definition of a palindrome according to Webster's Dictionary is: "Palindrome, n. (Gr., palindromos, running back; palin, again and dromos, a running): a word, verse or sentence that is the same when read backward or forward; as, madam, or Roma tibi subito motibus ibit amor."

There are benefits to reading something backwards. It is a positive brain exercise which enhances your conceptual ability. It stimulates the brain cells in a different way. For a pianist, reading the notes backwards makes you a better sight reader as well as increases your dexterity. The right and left hemispheres of the brain are both challenged when right and left hands play backwards. It is similar to the mental and physical challenge of writing your name with your left hand if you are right-handed or vice versa.

One of the first composers known to write a musical palindrome was Guillaume de Machaut (1304-1377). He was the leading composer of the ars nova in France. Machaut demonstrated sophisticated musical ingenuity in composing a tenor solo. Against the text "Ma fin est mon commencement et mon commencement ma fin" ("My end is my beginning and my beginning is my end"), in this composition a portion of the tenor line could be sung backwards as well as forward and sound the same. This famous musical curiosity is reproduced below.

Machaut, Ma fin est ma commencement

A semordnilap is something that makes sense either forward or backwards. An example is: the word 'stressed' spells 'desserts' backwards. It makes sense either way but a palindrome is the same either way like the word 'radar.'

Patriotic Semordnilap

Gail Smith

Palindrome

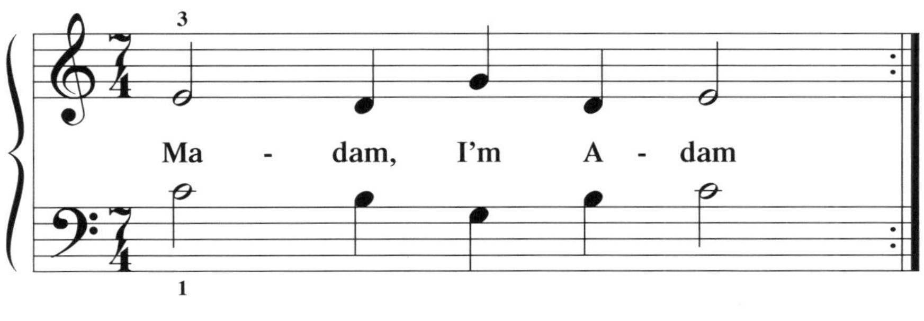

Reprinted by permission from Mel Bay's *Palindromes for Piano* (MB 20125, p. 3)

Canon Palindrome

Gail Smith

Chapter Eleven

Inverted Songs

Bach composed an inverted minuet that used the right hand melody in the left hand for the next minuet and then the left hand melody for the right hand of the other piece. The piece sounds good either way.

Minuet in G Minor

Allegretto (♩ = 128)

Johann Sebastian Bach

Minuet in G Minor

Allegretto (♩ = 128)

Johann Sebastian Bach

Chapter Twelve

Twelve Tone Songs

We have twelve different chromatic notes to use in a composition. If we tried to write a 12 tone row, that is, using each note only once until we use all twelve in the melody, it is called a 12 tone technique. Most compositions that are composed this way sound atonal. It is a compositional style originated by the composer Arnold Schonberg (1875-1951). What is interesting about this is the fact that there are four hundred and seventy-nine million, sixteen hundred different patterns of 12 numbers without repeating one single note. So you can see that the sky is the limit for the number of combinations that can go into a melody. Now take the twelve notes from middle C up to B and write them in any order without repeating one until all have been used. There are a few examples of different 12 tone rows for you to try.

Our Twelve Tones

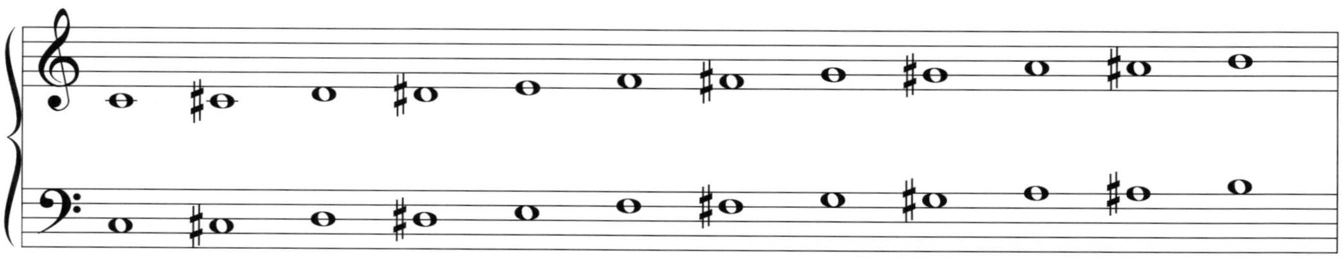

Random selection of notes

The Twelve Tone Row written backwards.
This is called a Retrograde.

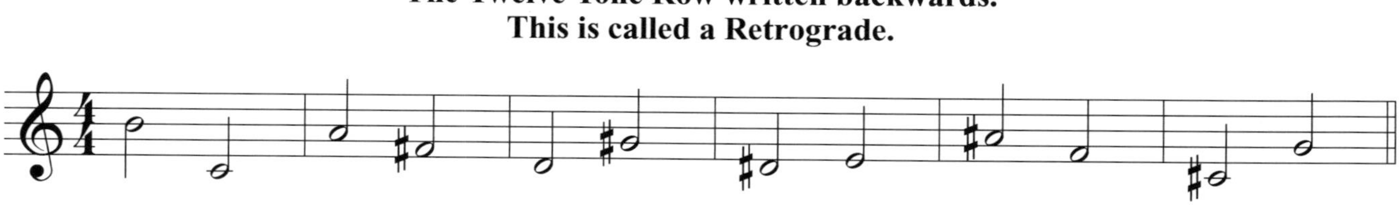

It can be fun to limit yourself to twelve notes and try to make it sound musical. Here are a few more examples.

1.

2.

Write an original random Twelve Tone Row.

Amy Beach's Ten Commandments for Composers

Amy Beach is known as "the first woman composer of America." She was born September 5, 1867 in Henniker, New Hampshire. She died December 27, 1944 in New York.

She composed hymns, piano solos, a piano concerto, numerous choral works, an opera, and the Gaelic Symphony, as well as many vocal and chamber works. In 1915, Beach gave an interview to the Los Angeles Examiner in which she cited "Ten Commandments for Young Composers":

1. Perfect the technique of composition, beginning with the simplest rudiments.

2. Begin with small things – ideas that can be expressed in small forms.

3. Develop all the possibilities of a small form.

4. Learn to employ as much variety in form as possible. Avoid becoming stereotyped in expressing melodic, harmonic, or rhythmic ideas.

5. Analyze the old masters, especially their examples in the same form (as, for a fugue, Bach's *Well-Tempered Clavier*).

6. Study the string quartets of Haydn, Mozart, and the early Beethoven; analyze and learn them by heart.

7. Listen to good string quartets at their rehearsals and concerts; take along a score and follow it.

8. Hear good choral music.

9. Learn the master works of the symphony as played by fine orchestras; be thorough in studying symphonic works.

10. Remember that technique is only a means to an end. You first must have something to say. "If you feel deeply and know to express what you feel, you make others feel."